Raindrops

POETRY *for* RAINY DAYS

Patricia Vollmann-Stock

Print ISBN 978-1-09836-280-5 | eBook ISBN 978-1-09836-281-2

Names, characters, places, and incidents are products of the author's imagination or are used fictitiously and are not to be construed as real. Any resemblance to actual events, locales, organizations, or persons, living or dead, is entirely coincidental.

The views expressed in these poems are from the imagination of the author.

PREFACE

I have always enjoyed reading and writing poetry ever since I was a young child. I was not an athletic child (measuring 4'10 in heels) nor could I paint, nor was I musically inclined. I wrote stories and poems. Poetry is a way for me to express my deepest emotions about life. Some of the poems I wrote was when I was younger, and they are sad and lonely and echo the low self-esteem of a young female's teenage years.

It is my hope that these poems will be read by others to know that we share the same experiences and feelings and that no one is alone. The beauty of poetry can be your friend and counsel when you need it the most.

Poetry is beautiful and can get a point across in an emotionally thought-provoking way. I have learned it is important to be honest with yourself, poetry is like gardening if you want it to have a beautiful result you must cultivate it and feed it.

I like to think about my poems and understand what I am trying to achieve before I can explain it to anyone else. I hope that these poems stir up deep feelings and capture all your senses. With comforting words, we can calm our central nervous systems and engage our minds to smell, taste and hear in wonderment of all life. May you learn to appreciate life, express gratitude, and learn the power of prayer in your own hearts.

I hope these poems bring you joy.

DEDICATION

For Ken who I love more every day
For Carlissa, Kelsea, Lillian, Abigail, and Edward and those who I
have not met yet. I loved you before I met you.

BIOGRAPHY

Patricia (Trish) Vollmann-Stock grew up in Maple Ridge in the
1970's and moved to Vancouver Island in 2006.
She is happily married to Ken and they live in Duncan BC as the
saying goes "If you are lucky enough to live by the sea, you are
lucky enough."
We share our condo with our two dogs, Jimmy and Joyce who are
chihuahua crosses.
I am a dog lover, trail walker, and rock gatherer.
I worked at the post office for 36 years, felt called to serve at church
and now I work in retail.
I am a proud Mother, grandmother, and friend.
I love my family and learn from them every day.
These days I feel "called" to pray with my pen.

RAINDROPS
TABLE OF CONTENTS

Spring

Summer

Autumn

Winter

Spring

RAINDROPS

I am grateful to be in the presence of the rain.
Creating vibrations on the earth, rehydration.
Earthworms surface. They are unaware if this is the trickery of a
bird drumming his feet or the soft rain tapping on the grass, or the
heartbeat of God.
None the wiser they stretch from their muddy slumber to soak in the
day and hear the music.
Refreshment
I stand by a tree in awe of the droplets soaking the earth.
Listening to the varying sounds of the drops as they collide with
whatever is in its way.
Playing different melodies, pre-orchestrated thousands of times
by kismet.
The veiled sounds of the cello rain are muffled in the flower beds.
The exaggerated harmonic tones of the woodwind section vibrate
through the pines.
I match my breath note by note whilst the orchestra plays on.

THE WATER WILL POUR THREE TIMES

My mother dresses me in crisp white linen,
The gown recovered from her wedding dress.
She and I are adorned in pearls and lace.
She has my favorite blanket.
Glass windows make prisms on the floor.
It smells of wood and smoky perfume.
Angels dance on the ceiling.
The organ thumps. A man cradles me in his arms.
I stare at his bearded face and grab at his beads; He takes them off
his neck.
They are cold and smooth on my gums.
He rubs oil on my head and says a prayer.
My parents peer.
On the ceiling above me cherubs laugh.
Cold water cascades over my small blonde head
Again
And the again.
I drift to sleep.
Somehow changed,
Sanctified and whole.

MOM

She wore aprons that she had sewn in pastel colors of mauve
and pink.
It was her spiritual attire.
She could laugh with a generous spirit.
And was truly clothed in strength and dignity.
She was our light for all generations to follow.
Her calming smile and gentle touch
Could see the good in everyone.
Through all her struggles and joys
Through her grey eyes with flecks of violet and amber

IMPERFECT PRAISE

Prayer need not be perfect.
Praise can be laughing with a friend.
Or tear soaked.
Face
Feelings imperishable
Take on new life, naturally.
Ordinary has vanished.
Heart learns new ways to love.
At peace
And heard.

THE MAN FROM DEVON

I do not think I could.
Ever understand how.
Someone would want to lay down and stare into the forest,
Until I saw your eyes.
In your eyes I saw a shade of green that
God created just for you.
A color between slate and sage
A color so captivating that I was thrown off balance.
And deeply aroused.
Yet, I refuse to look away.
In your eyes I see a mossy garden bed
And I yearn to snuggle.
Enraptured by the green.
Blissful quiet and besotted.
I see how it is possible to want.
To be lost there.
And never be found.

I WANT TO BELONG.

The trees sparkle with the kiss of rain.
As I stare out at the terrain
The sunshine warms my soul.
And touches my heart like a newborn foal.
Each day is a precious gift,
A chance to give our lives new lift.
Forgive all that is behind.
And a chance of joy to fill our mind.
Confess and release your plenty burden.
Your excuses too as we have heard them.
I ask to be paroled from doubt.
About myself I once cared about
I do not wish to boast or brag.
I yearn for calm and hold up high.
To be at peace in my own head
To feel comfort and not the dread
This is my prayer, mantra, chant.
To be happy and remove the cant.
What did I do to feel such mistrust?
Bound by guilt, lies hurts and lust.
Forgive myself relax and love.
Please pour out your forgiveness from above
Each step I take I fear I will fail.
And self-fulfillment will avail.
I must not hate myself no more.
This need to stop my life down the drain I pour.
The clouds now float softly by
To dry my tears, no more to cry

WHERE THE LILIES AND ROSES GROW

Many days I feel disconnected from the vibrant spirit filled
ministries of the prophets and apostles of biblical times.
Where are the miracles?
Am I looking too hard, or am I?
Not looking at all.
Faith, yet still a mysterious word on paper to be discovered
and explained.
But it cannot be sorted with a few keystrokes and a dictionary.
My God is always involved in creation.
This is ordinary providence.
My faith and love cannot be described in a single moment.
But rather in all moments, and always.
My mind is a seesaw.
When I focus on my faith and trust my fears and worries go down
When I look into the eyes of my grandchildren, I feel hope.
In my field of despair
Where the lilies and roses grow

GERBERA DAISY

Bright and majestic
Proud
Like the face of a lion with his mane
Intimidating to other flowers with less beauty
And impressive to prospective bees.

Hues of orange, pink, red yellow and
Striped ones like hard Christmas ribbon candy
Each bearing messages.
Of love, grace, and cheer
Just like our God

SPRINGTIDE

The renewal of life,
God's creation is animated in a myriad of hue,
Nature awakens its sleep filled eyes of dew.
Trees start to deliciously stretch towards the celestial sphere.
Sprouting seeds, animals drawing near.

The sunshine tenderly wraps us in warmth and light.
Roots anchoring down with all their might.
Water, sun, and soil
The holy trinity of spring.
The first stage of life that creation and creator bring.
The season of joy and change to begin.
To grow above, below, within
The chilled star nights and delights of frost.
And joy the showers.
The landscape glossed.

Blossoms, buds, and heavenly scents
God's watercolor enchantments
Cherished aspirations become unclouded.
Renewal reconciled now undoubted.

OUR LORD OUR GARDENER.

A gentle tug on my branches allows me to breathe.
Free of fear I am at last unsheathed.
Wholesome balance free of blight.
Space and time to meander, unfold.
Great observers amend and mold.

My fronds advance with poise and ease.
No breaking but oscillating in the breeze.
The gardener allows my own time to render.
The harmony flow, the careful mender.
The quiet movements into shape,
Bring stamina for limbs to drape.

I feel the power deep into my root.
As my trunk begins to transmute.
Heartfelt thanks I leave this space,
Gardeners work complete – a smiling face.

Summer

OLD LEIGH

It was months ago I walked arm in arm with my love through the seashore at Leigh-On- Sea down to the cockle sheds. The breeze was the perfect temperature that day and it caressed my face and ran its fingers through my hair. I had goosebumps of delight.

You could smell the salt in the air and the hint of cinnamon sugar from the mini donuts beside the cockle sheds. We were laughing at the silly seagulls performing air acrobatics as they practiced dive bombing the fishermen's' nets on shore. The seagull's caws were of merriment as the water lapped up debris scooping it back into the ocean.

In the distance was music coming from the pub below. I imagined the bittersweet taste of a creamy shandy as we made out way down on the cobble stone steps. It was a perfect day the kind of day you dial up in your memory when you are at the dentist or locked out of your car.

UNRETURNED LOVE FROM PSALM 96: 11-12

Let the heavens rejoice, let the earth be glad.
Let the sea resound, and all that is in it.
Let the fields be jubilant, and everything in them.
Let all the trees of the forest sing for joy.

There is no appeal to the sympathy of nature, unrequited love, nor
the mercy of the hot sun.
Rain and tears calm her frayed nerves and cool her body down.
Once the cloudbursts subside, the wrath of the milky way
draws nigh.
Her heart bursts open with Orion crushing crimson berries
staining violet.
Fermenting and pouring the first taste of merlot to touch her sweet
lips a lustful thrill.
A forbidden love that has driven her **mad**
The lavender coloured mystery of the sky with swirls of vermillion
takes her breath away.
Inhaling and drawing air deep into her bosom and all her hurting
parts, crushed like Orion's fruit.
Scattering the wispy clouds into a frenzy of colour into a
purple **plaid**.
Let the heavens rejoice, let the earth be glad.

The ocean lets his voice be heard with his roaring thunder.
Clapping his hands to summon nearby nimbus stratus.
He has no pity on the wench who has her head in the clouds.
The cold dark depths of blue keep his demeanour unknown.
Mystery surrounds his vast uncovered pools.
Until provoked he beats his drum into a **fit**
Mocking her at pitiful sight of falling in love
Knowing she will be disappointed.
But loving her anyways as she can not **quit**.
Let the sea resound, and all that is in it.

Sing and be glad like the buttercups bursting into smiles.
The orange marigolds turn upwards to kiss the sky.
The stinging of her tears makes pollen-streaked tears on her face.
Love is never wasted just misplaced.
A life with kindness and adoration is the blossom to the **stem.**
all the flowers bask in her radiant smile and flowing hair.
her daydreams of wishes and kisses fill the air.
she caresses each flower, and each are a precious **gem.**
let the fields be jubilant, and everything in them.

she finds comfort and wisdom by conversing with the trees.
the shrubs her brothers who comfort her needs
the ever greens stand firm and proud.
and remind the lovely child to stand as tall.
loving everyone completely is not a **toy.**
nor to be cast aside or outgrown
love is to be treasured when truly found.
not to be wasted for the lust of a **boy**
let all the trees of the forest sing for joy.

THROW THE BALL!

I can not write; I am a dog. I say everything you need to hear with my eyes.

If I could write you a letter describing, you it would be complete. It would be honest and the entire truth.

Sometimes I see you crying alone. I do not know why you are sad maybe you try to hard to please everyone.

All you really need to do is.

Throw the ball.

I know you love this game! Truth is I do it all for you.

You seem distracted sometimes you throw the ball to far or you do not pick it up right away when I throw it at your feet.

I know to always please you. I do it all for you.

You keep my water and food bowl full; I keep your heart full.

You are my universe.

Well, you and my ball.

You are all you need to be to me you are perfect.

Let this be your centering prayer.

Love Jimmy

SCOOP

I looked up.
to the large
double coop
chocolate chip
melted peppermint.
brazil nut
ice cream cone.
my mouth watered.
my eyes bulged.
the sign read fifteen cents.
as I gazed longingly at the lush feast, so delicious, tantalizing.
I reached into the pocket of my jeans.
with teary eyes
hungry tummy
and a broken heart
I sadly searched.
and could only find.
a dime.

HUES OF TWILIGHT

The weary sun winked over the horizon conveying soft diffused light
in every direction, cueing the darkness to arrive.
Casting shadows of the trees, melting into the water is exit is ever
so grand.
Magenta tails on fluffy clouds, watercolors of amber and tangerine
infuse the pale sky.
Just like a million times before
Offering the onlookers, a ballet of hues and swirls
And pausing the business of our existence.
Marking the end of another day, a chance to reflect like the sun in all
we hold dear.

FIBER

Walking is fiber for the soul.
Fresh air is the only detox you need.
From the sludge in your mind

Happiness is the warmth of the earth.
And the pure joy of being alive.
Go out into the beauty and all.
The smells of creation
Praise God for the many blessings
Do not let life pass by.
Whilst sitting in the dark
Go into the sunshine.
Feel the majesty.
Our savior was born.
Outdoors.

COLD ROCKS

As I wander through the words in search of nature reclaiming herself
I pray for glimpses of spring.
Undisturbed and underground during her winter slumber
The earth is hushed and at rest.
I remove my shoes when I reach the brook.
Fragments of my childhood flow through my body as my feet
touch the
Cold rocks
I am an adventurous explorer of the unknown.
My restless spirit has pushed me to new heights for renewal.
There is no end to the happiness my body is willing to bear.
I am in my sanctuary.
It is here in the stillness, that my Lord breaks through the noise of
my mind
And allows me to hear, feel and come alive.

HAPPY HERON

Sitting motionless on the edge of the shallow water,
Crouching down his ashen feathers camouflaged in the dreary
swamp grass.
He recognizes an opportunity.
Careful calculation he awaits.
The perfect timing to spear his prey.
He arises with graceful determination, his long legs in
ballerina pose.
He drops a bug into the tranquil water to attract a fish.
With joy in his saffron eyes, he launches his head down into the
cool waters.
Independent and patient
Alone in the quiet
He eats his catch.

RIVER ROAD

It lays between the Fraser River and the Golden Ears.
The twin summit that tosses about the sun like a game of catch at
days end.
It is where my world began, with grass-stained feet, dirty hands and
sun burned belly.
It is where I learned to love and cry and that pet rabbits die, as do
Moms and Dads.
And holes are left in heart and clothes and that life is not over
but changed.
It is where crepe paper streamers adorn bicycles, and first place
ribbons are bright blue.
Nestled in the maples and pines we played until dark, we ran
through puddles and fashioned helicopters from the seeds of
sycamore trees.
Throwing them high and jumping up to follow their descent.
Racing and chasing butterflies, picking dandelions, and making
salads and potions fit for a king.
Everything belongs.
Our imaginations bursting in love with life itself.
An innocence I crave and long for before the enormity of the world
taught us how to see.
Turning upside down to the what the view is from another
perspective. Laying on dewy lawns, dashing through garden
sprinklers, listening to the sounds, and taking in the smells of wood
smoke from the Hammond Mill.
We were scratched and scraped and covered in berry splatter and
wore our dirty band aids like badges of honor.
We were pink popsicle eating warriors, and misfits, outcasts
of our youth who were unaware that we were a small part of a
bigger mystery.
We lived in amazement and were steadied and cherished and formed
one by one by life on River Road.

PRAIRIE SKY

Every sun kissed day.
The bright canola will fill the fields.
My hands will touch the green alfalfa.
And a happiness will come over me.
Like a warm chinook wind.
I must close my eyes to take it in
The splendor, the beauty
I hope that you can also taste the sweet almondy joy of the
Saskatoon berry,
And pause.
To smile at the golden bearded gnomes(wheat)
Blowing in the fields.
the infinity of the indigo prairie sky
the plunging chasms and shape shifting sand dunes.
for such a creation, such beauty here on earth
is Saskatchewan.

Autumn

MOON AT NIGHT

The moon is not afraid of the dark
She wears her silver stockings and arrives before the dawn,
She hangs in the sky without a care in the world.
She sees dark deeds, and weary travelers and wolves who choose
to howl.
She is blamed for madness and rage.
And glorified for babies born and other promises she did not make.
She hears confessions.
And tears of all sorts and takes them all in stride.
She always shows her face, even under a blanket of cloud.
She does not hide.
She is love or feared but she does not care.
She is willing to be night's constant companion as she is.
Not afraid

THE LIFE OF WATER

The rain droplets on the windshield
It was the big race.
Which one would win?
Finally, they reach the bottom.
Sticking to other droplets along their way
Splashing through puddles
Catching rain on my tongue
Rinsing and drinking
From the garden hose
Soaking wet
Splashing
Into the hot bath
Scrubbing
Warming up tiny hands
Sitting at the dining table
Water glasses full
Digging out ice
With fingers
That were once splashed.
With holy water
The water soaking into the earth.
Rising to heaven
And returning cycling from the clouds
As a glass of water
That may be.
For
A great leader of our country.

THE WIND HAS MUCH TO SAY.

The wind has much to say.
If I listen
Often unadorned she is quiet, a gentle breeze of natural movements
of the air around us.
A pleasant feeling
She carries seeds and little birds for as many miles as she sees fit.
An angel with unfurled wings and gentle movements
Time traveler
She powers boats and lifts our spirits, parting clouds to show off
blue skies.
But she is a force like no other a jealous lover.
With a mind of her own and she cannot be tamed
Often a tempest she flattens buildings, wrecks ship, and erodes the
very earth where she dwells.
She commands the trees to dance.
Her loud voice howling. She is furious, she is fierce.
She hides, invisible to anyone who tries to see her.
We only hear her whispers and screams.
And long for her presence in the heat.
But she has other plans.

WHISPERED INVOCATIONS

Alone, on the stump of a tree examining the new shoots of live that
come from its hardened trunk,
Reminding me that we can return, regenerate, and grow stronger.
I hear the gentleness of the breeze in the beauty of a laurel tree and a
sparrow summersaulting in the sky. This is the freedom that I desire,
this is the simple yet curious landscape that my heart requires.
There is no measure of time in counting on a clock, but the beauty
in the dichotomy of light and dark that nature provides. I feel
absolution here in this place from the chill on my face and the air all
around me.
I watch families walking together, the joy of parents walking with
children, babies wrapped up in prams and older folks, shaky on the
trail navigating each step with their canes, their staffs for comfort
and protection and they wander through the forest in the midst of a
garden landscape.
I have returned to an area that is pure, and at peace with creation.
Every day I walk a path of present desolation and future glory. This
is the place where I find my faith and where you find me.
It is here where my soul finds healing, where I soften, and where
I pray.

CAMPAIGN SIGNS

Shiny promises on wooden signs.
Great bright colors and nice straight lines
But do you know anything that is true.
Why do you have hated in you?
How can you say it will all change?
Its only chaos you rearrange.
You are not willing to pay a price.
No ultimate sacrifice
It is hard to find a true leader.
Not some self-fulfilling gossip feeder
Change will be one by one.
Someone who is real will get it done.
I worry for the world today.
But I trust the one after the one who prepared the way.

THICKET IN THE HALF LIGHT

The evergreens stood proud,
rising from the earth like a menorah.
A scene from Babylon.
The emanation from the coruscation of
the sunbeams casting shadows on the trunks.
to prepare a lined pathway to the divine.
The sun teasing its way through to
make its debut tricking and captivating each person.
who cast their eyes upon the splendour?
Asherah herself was jealous and overwhelmed by
the quietude and unadulterated beauty
as the forest lay before her.
The nymph was no match to rise to the heights of
the graceful presence in her sight, so she
turned away from the grove, she blushed as
she turned her head back around one last time like a
parting lover for one more eyeful,
her faery wings unfurled, and she flew away.
Believing that night and day no longer at battle, have
compromised and settled on.
this one perfect moment.

AUTUMN PLAYGROUND

Any day now
The chimney smokes.
Wafts overhead.
Smudging the sky
Smells of sweet cherry and hickory.
And savory will rise up.
A mischievous crow calls out.
And the chitter of the spotted towhee.
Fills the cool air.
The dark eyed junco hides in the brush.
Dormant and still
The pendulous leaves of copper and amber
Hang overhead.
Squirrels rush around busily.
Making autumn last
Before the cold dark days ahead
And are merrily thankful.
For such creation
Out of the harvest
Which is desired
A prayer for us all.

FORECAST IS FOR UNSTABLE CONDITIONS

The weather was superb on my wedding day, sunshine in the short-term forecast. I married well, a rich man whose yacht was as excessive and pretentious as his heart. There were clear conditions and great visibility for the short term. The weather report was predictable and reliable -- just as I was to, he. The wind direction changed the day one rain drop became a salty tear and the clouds came rushing in. This was the day I found my voice and stood firm in the high winds not backing away from the cruel harsh pounding of the hailstorms he spewed on me, no longer a trickle but a full harsh storm. I piled cigarettes one by one in the ashtray waiting for the clouds to break, but they closed in all around me. His hands grew as cold as the weather system as he wrapped his hands around my throat choking out the daylight with his winters grip. As I fell to the ground, I could see the once glimmer of light through the window, now just a dark low pressure as the barometer fell as did I.

CHIMNEY POTS

Even the name makes me smile.
The proud terra cotta soldiers with halo rings around their feet
drawn in the frosty roof.
How I long to stand beside them twirling an umbrella like a baton.
Merrily dancing with the screeves
Conversing with Mary and Bert
Laughing at the seagulls flailing in the wind unable to land
As we stand tall, unmoved, unshaken for the slow burning fire in the
hearth below.
Cancels all doubt.
That we are firmly attached.

IT WAS EARLY.

the arms of the clock reaching out to the 5.
of course, the day has already been heard.
by birds chirping.
Imagining mice scurried about
Hiding from owls
Perched in trees.
The first rays of sunlight
Scattered in the atmosphere.
And all the leaves and branches
Frozen in time
The frost covered pathways.
Nature's tinsel hung in trees.
Sometimes I only need to stand and look.
Wherever I am
To be blessed.

SQUIRREL

Capricious little scamp.
Unknowingly planting trees of tomorrow with his caches of nuts and
seeds with the few he has left behind.
He pauses and contemplates the philosophy of his day. Ever curious,
ever bold. He practices being quiet and mature, but his nature is
eccentric and eclectic.
His translucent coat taking on the green light filtering through
the trees.
His meditation is swiftly interrupted by a nearby bird drawing closer
to his treasures. He chitters and scurries in circles on the forest
floor and he means every word he is chattering to his foe.
Squirrels are the sprites of the woodlands and when they react it is
with cause; it makes sense to them and they believe in themselves
with all their hearts.
He is so worthy of his fluffy tale and pixie face and is fearless
and fun.

Winter

TAX COLLECTORS, FISHERMEN AND THIEVES

John was a writer.
It has been told.
He did not hide behind a mask.
His foxy shape and pleasant face were all he needed.
There were no mirrors.
Only lakes for reflection
And reflection is all that is needed.

Who will follow who will stay close?
They lived in crooked trees.
They gathered in the town square.
They range the triangle bell and sit at square tables to form a circle.
A strange shape these twelve, each with a tale of their own

The Lion of Judah appeared, not by grand entrance but rather meek
and humble like a lamb.
The twelve longed to be nearby.
They did not know what was to come.
He called them all by name and told them to take nothing with them
for the upcoming journey.
The circus had come to town.
They ate and drank and danced with jesters, fenced with fools, and
cycled with clowns.

Simon the hare appeared all in a flutter.
His usual intense self, dragging a washboard behind him.
His two unlikely band mates were Thunderous James a fiddle playing
beaver and Andrew the rhythm keeper of the band.
Matthew the disciple weasel was asked to join the group, why would
anyone want him there?
They were unlikely leaders, but they were wanted there.
In the crowd was Thomas the goat full of doubt exclaiming that the
day would not be a good one.

No one could assure him that everything was fine.
They shared a meal, and the mood was somber, the lion explained
that things would change.
But how?
The mood changed with every performance from light to dark and
from beautiful to ugly.
The big top curtain was torn in two.
Pandemonium broke out.
The band broke up.
The circus was over.
There was a great mess left behind.
How would they overcome the tragedies who was going to keep the
show on the road?
They all felt great fear and doubt and guilt for their selfish ways.

It was three long days.
Whilst out for a walk a fan of the circus, a woman no less came across
a glowing light.
She fell to her knees.
Was this the Lion? But he had been killed, murdered for his
blasphemy, his lies and stories that made entitled people feel small
and threatened by his teachings of goodness.

FIRST SNOW

She has arrived with the radiance of a new bride.
Her veil and train cascading over the pathways, hills, and trees.
Graceful and poised her elegance captivates the eyes of those who
behold her.
Whisper quiet she drifts into our day and we are overcome
with somnolence.
The air is woodsy and fresh and smells of cedar and pine terpenes
occupy our space.
A virgin's descent with each frozen petal touching down.
The sky is mesmerizing as the flakes meander to the ground.
The pearly ground is tranquil and at peace.
Hushed and pristine
In this one moment of time.

BLACK HOODED FELLOWS

The dark eyed junco is more than just a neat flashy sparrow.
Hopping along gleaning food from twigs and leaves low in
the underbrush.
He is the freedom of spirit.
Coming to announce the winter season, the arrival of the
Christ child.
His happy melody signing truth and hope.
He is Heaven's piccolo
Tiny and full of life

A NOTE, A SHOE, A PENNY

In our world with mysteries too marvelous to understand,
We see what we want to see with our eyes.
But our hearts see differently.

Sometimes our angels fly so close to earth.
That they drop something
A note, a shoe, a penny.

In their haste to check on us
And leave us a reminder of them drawing near.
So, when you see that out of place item.
On the ground or in your path
You have been visited.

WORKS AS WELL IF YOU READ IT FROM THE BOTTOM.

It was there the moment you were born.
It lingers on long after you die.
Not everything about it has been written.
Not everything about it has been said.
The full magnitude of it has not been felt.
It arrives bound up inside a tear.
It bursts fiercely out of your eyes.
Streaming down
Heart pounding
No where to hide.
And why would you hide.
It is more powerful than the rush of the ocean.
Hotter than scarlet flames
It lives outside of you.
If you let it, it lives inside of you.
It is Love.

THE STEAMER TRUNK

We smashed the lock on the steamer trunk.
Its blue walls held skeleton keys, perhaps the keys to the trunk,
manila envelopes frayed at the corners,
embroidered baby clothes with pink piping, neatly wrapped in
tissue paper,
baby blankets, two worn, one new, holy in more than the literal
sense. They were.
McCall's' and Butterick maternity dress patterns, the beige tissue
almost faded away,
greyish brown utility shoes size 5 insoles still intact,
dried flowers and leaves pressed between wax paper neatly placed on
top of
black and white photos from kodak film, white borders, her wry
smile, and her hands cradling her.
pregnant belly, dated 1955.
Green twist ties were bundled together like hay bales on the prairie,
Hair ribbons in hues of dusty rose with eyelet lace and
gingham fabrics,
Avon perfume samples in delicate glass bottles, half full but
well-preserved,
embossed greeting cards from England with cancelled stamps, with
glitter and round-faced.
children holding balloons with happy greetings of Mother's Day,
and one
unopened card.
Children's drawings, well-scribbled crayon, with "Mommy" written
by adult hand dated 1967.
One blank piece of paper.
Hospital bracelets wrapped in tissue with locks of hair,
two of them with baby books with heights and weights and
events recorded,
and one way at the bottom of the trunk,
the bracelet, the photos, and the adoption papers,
my sister,
lovingly hidden.

RIBBON OF MEMORY

White wisp of a cloud, a hint, a fleeting trace
A precious heaven scent memory ribbon that time erased.
A laugh a smile my eyes now low
From once a hearty glance once flow.
Very quiet and locked inside.
Once upright, honest full of pride.
I cannot recall the stove left on
Its noontime but my curtains drawn.
My precious child is still in school.
But she is 61 so am I the fool?
I think I heard the doorbell ring.
Is mid July I wish for spring.
I act out and cause you grief.
But nature is my memory thief.
I wait now or I wander off.
Not an easy ailment like a cough.
We all wish we could find the cure.
Alzheimer's robbed us the filthy boor.

Praise ye the LORD. Praise ye the LORD from the heavens: praise him in the heights.
Praise ye him, all his angels: praise ye him, all his hosts.
Praise ye him, sun and moon: praise him, all ye stars of light.
Praise him, ye heavens of heavens, and ye waters that be above the heavens.

PRAISE YE

On this most holy night
The laundry remains unsorted, in a pile.
And a few are out on the Christmas tree lights.
Yet we praise ye the Lord, praise ye the lord from the heavens praises
him in the heights.

Her back is sore from stacking wood.
To keep the fireplace lit, she works so hard but never brags
nor boasts.
But praises ye him, all his angels praise ye him all his hosts.

The cookies baked, the gravy renders.
In her weary mind she knows everything is alright
She praises ye him, sun and moon, praise him, all ye starts of light.

Her body tired a tear she wipes away.
She will not see her bed nor bath until after eleven.
But she does not forget to
Praise him, ye heavens of heavens and ye waters that be above
the heavens.

Rattled, shattered she can not calm her mind.
Stress closing her throat like a strangling hand.
Finger pointing, whispers, blame.
Shame
Despite the worries of the days
Grant her rest
Be acceptable and at peace.
And trust that your life will take shape into who you are meant to be.

ST STEPHENS CEMETERY

Chilly December
The sky has two faces.
The sun so low
Just waking up.
The cold moon aglow with silver
Finishing her last lap.

In the cemetery nestled below
So many stories
Smells of sweet pipe smoke and cherry pies.
And laughter in the trees.

Memories of weddings, dances and toasts
Church picnics with chicken and
All those potato salads.

The flower petals take sail.
In the gentle breezes.
All life holy
The souls live on in story and son.

New water is poured on the old stones.
The marble and limestone
And worn lettering.
The letter T
Broken
Hardly legible in the dawn
But their lives
Carried in our hearts.
Generation to generation.

HE WALKS.

Standing at the corner
Fingers yellowed from cigarettes.
Puts the smoking butt towards
His dirty beard and
Decaying teeth
Draws a shallow breath.
And throws the lit snub.
Towards the ground
And it smolders.
He turns around.
And his many frayed layers
And crippled abused body
Make it difficult to walk.
So, he shuffles.
And groans
And stands at the next corner.
Hand out
Body slumped.
Looking for a dollar
Or a coffee or a meal
He gets smears.
And cursing
Until a man
With holes in hands
Takes his arm.
And he walks.